Hairy Frogfish

by Grace Hansen

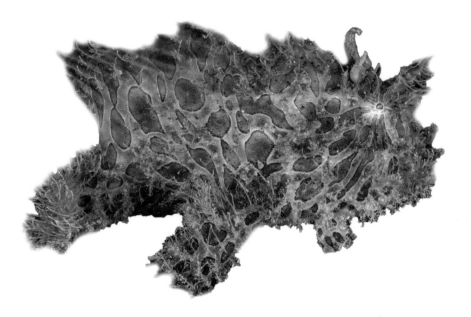

Abdo Kids Jumbo is an Imp-int of Abdo Kids
abdobooks.com

abdobooks.com

Published by Abdo Kids, a division of ABDO, P.O. Box 398166, Minneapolis, Minnesota 55439.
Copyright © 2021 by Abdo Consulting Group, Inc. International copyrights reserved in all countries.
No part of this book may be reproduced in any form without written permission from the publisher.
Abdo Kids Jumbo™ is a trademark and logo of Abdo Kids.

Printed in the United States of America, North Mankato, Minnesota.

052020

092020

THIS BOOK CONTAINS RECYCLED MATERIALS

Photo Credits: Alamy, BluePlanet Archive, iStock, Minden Pictures, Shutterstock

Production Contributors: Teddy Borth, Jennie Forsberg, Grace Hansen
Design Contributors: Dorothy Toth, Pakou Moua

Library of Congress Control Number: 2019956568
Publisher's Cataloging-in-Publication Data

Names: Hansen, Grace, author.
Title: Hairy frogfish / by Grace Hansen
Description: Minneapolis, Minnesota : Abdo Kids, 2021 | Series: Spooky animals | Includes online resources
    and index.
Identifiers: ISBN 9781098202538 (lib. bdg.) | SBN 9781098203511 (ebook) | ISBN 9781098204006 (Read-
    to-Me ebook)
Subjects: LCSH: Frogfishes--Juvenile literature. | Marine fishes--Juvenile literature. | Marine fishes—
    Behavior--Juvenile literature. | Curiosities and wonders--Juvenile literature.
Classification: DDC 596.018--dc23

Table of Contents

Hairy Frogfish

Hairy frogfish live in warm waters around the world. They mostly **inhabit** shallow areas. These areas can be sandy, rocky, or filled with **coral reefs**.

4

North America

Europe

Asia

Africa

South America

Australia

■ hairy frogfish range

5

Hairy frogfish are not really hairy. They are covered in **spinules**. Spinules can be long, short, or almost invisible.

7

A frogfish is a type of anglerfish. The anglerfish got its name for the fishing rod-like **spinule** above its mouth. It is called an illicium. At the end of it is an esca. This attracts **prey**.

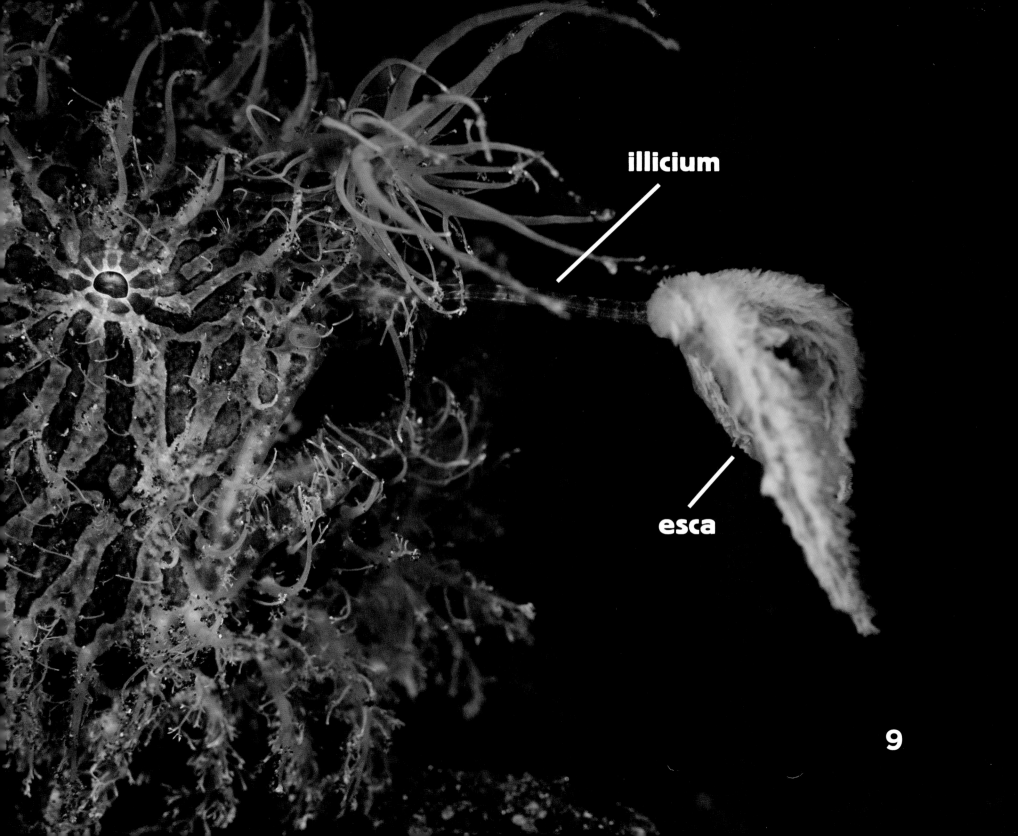

illicium

esca

9

Hairy frogfish can be many colors.

This is because they change to

blend in with their surroundings.

11

Hairy frogfish have small, round bodies. They can grow up to 10 inches (25.4 cm) long.

Hunting & Food

Though they are small, frogfish are **fierce** hunters. They either follow **prey** or **lure** it with their escas. When they are ready to pounce, they move very fast.

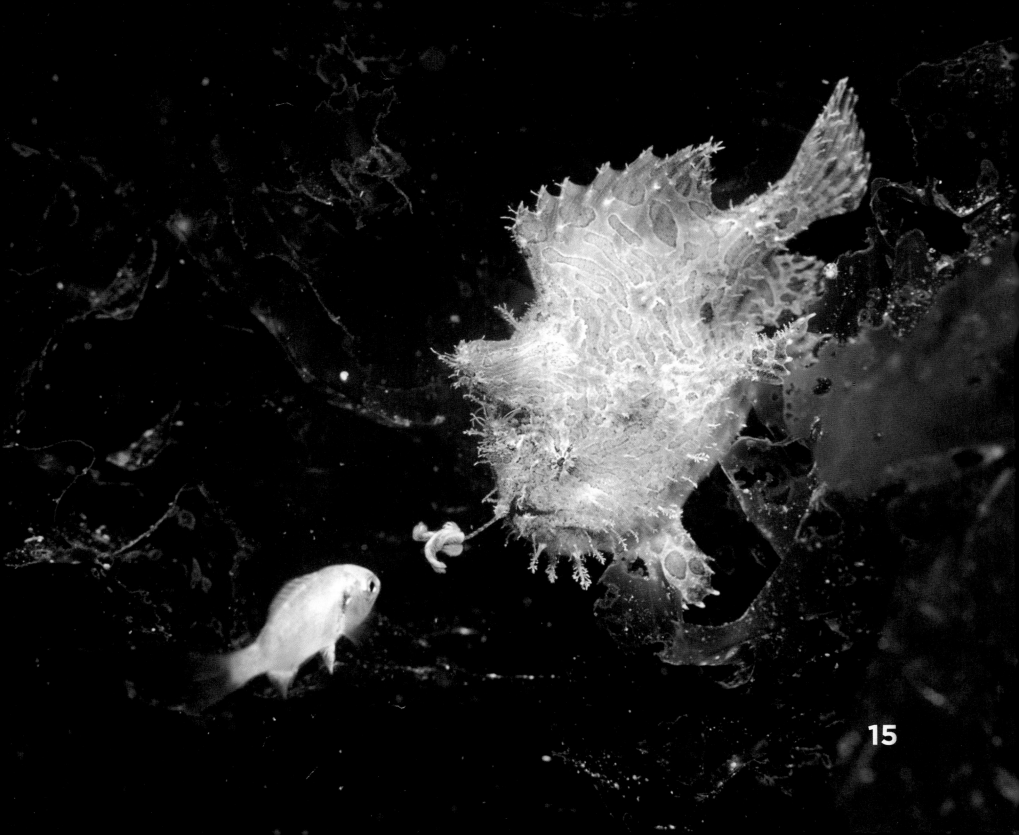

A hairy frogfish's mouth can open wide. The fish can suck in and swallow **prey** twice its size!

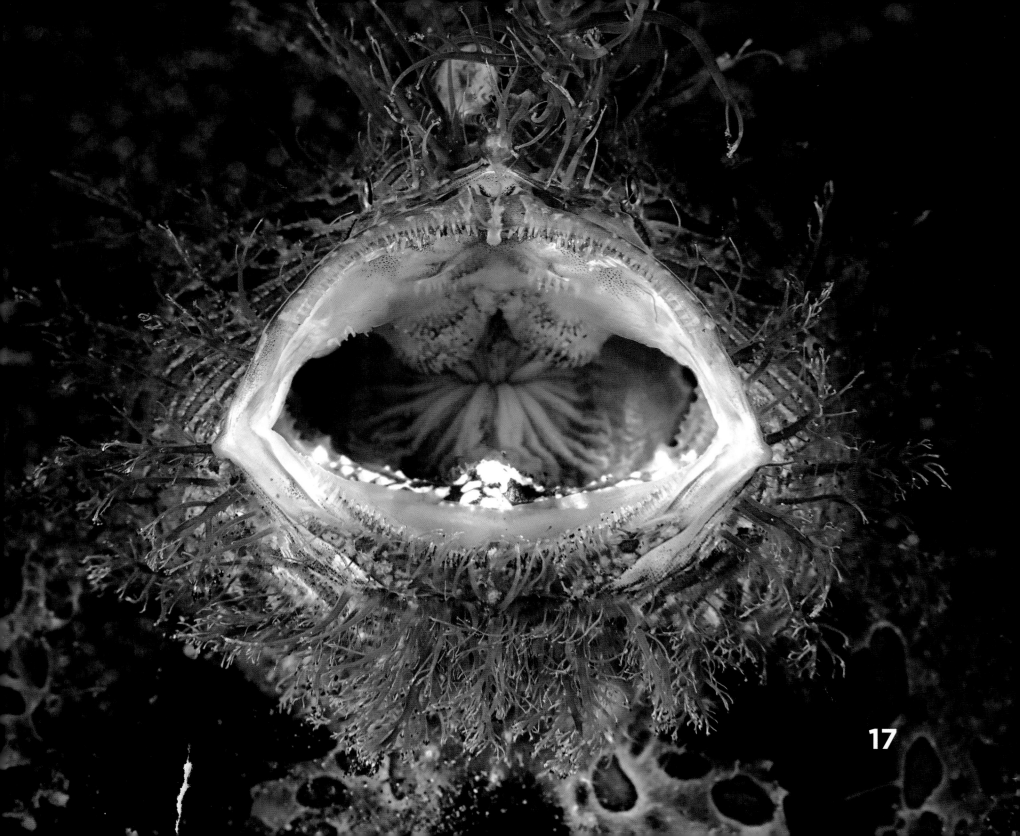

17

Baby Hairy Frogfish

A female hairy frogfish can produce up to 180,000 eggs at once. She releases the eggs into the water. A male **fertilizes** the eggs.

18

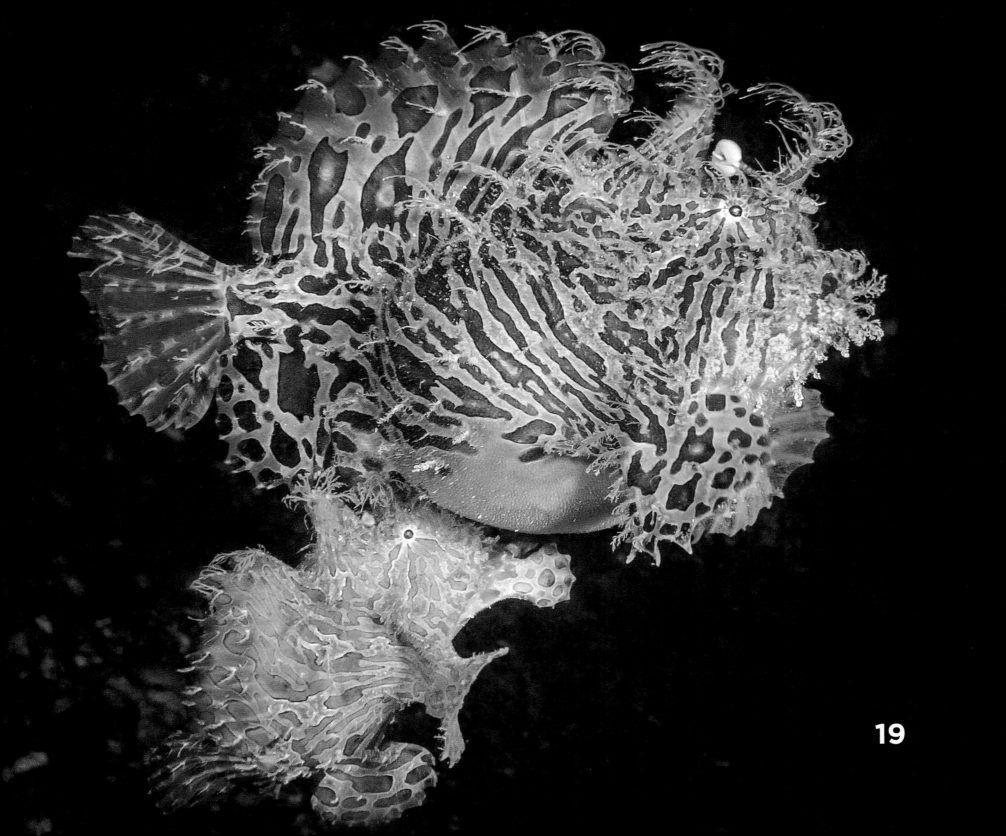

19

When the eggs are ready to hatch, they sink to the ocean floor. Newly-hatched frogfish are tiny. They hide among plants and coral until they are bigger.

More Facts

- Hairy frogfish don't really swim. Instead, they use their fins to push themselves along the ocean floor.

- Escas attract **prey** because they look like small animals, like worms.

- Male hairy frogfish are smaller than females.

Glossary

coral reef – a ridge or grouping of coral that lies in warm, shallow water. Coral are tiny, soft-bodied animals that look like plants.

fertilize – to make able to produce babies.

fierce – wild and dangerous.

inhabit – to live in.

lure – to attract and catch fish or other animals.

prey – an animal being hunted by another animal for food.

spinule – a small hair- or thorn-like body feature on some animals.

23

Index

Abdo Kids
ONLINE
FREE! ONLINE MULTIMEDIA RESOURCES

Visit **abdokids.com**
to access crafts, games,
videos, and more!

Use Abdo Kids code
SHK2538
or scan this QR code!

24